LEVEL
2

Wild Cats

Elizabeth Carney

NATIONAL
GEOGRAPHIC

Washington, D.C.

A big thank-you to Anne Montero's class for sharing their excellent questions about wild cats! – E. C.

This British English edition published in 2017 by Collins, an imprint of HarperCollins*Publishers*, The News Building, 1 London Bridge Street, London. SE1 9GF.

Browse the complete Collins catalogue at
www.collins.co.uk

ISBN: 978-0-00-826658-5
US Edition ISBN: 978-1-4263-2677-6

The author and publisher gratefully acknowledge the expert content review of this book by Linda Sweanor, wild cat biologist and past president of Wild Felid Research and Management Association, and the literacy review of this book by Mariam Jean Dreher, professor of reading education, University of Maryland, College Park.

Printed in China by RR Donnelley APS

Author's Note
When referring to the young of wild cats, many biologists use the terms "cub" and "kitten" interchangeably. Others, however, make a distinction between the terms, using "cub" for the young of big cats and "kitten" for the young of other wild cats, especially the smallest species. For the purpose of this book, the term "cub" is used to refer to the young of all wild cat species. The cover features a Eurasian lynx. On the title page, an ocelot slinks through the jungle. A caracal is shown on the table of contents.

Photo Credits
Cover, Jasper Doest/Foto Natura/Minden Pictures; 1 (CTR), Frans Lanting/National Geographic Creative; 3 (LO RT), Eric Isselee/Shutterstock; 4-5 (CTR), Jason Prince/Dreamstime.com; 6 (CTR), iStock.com/Dirk Freder; 7 (UP), Andrew Schoeman/Minden Pictures; 7 (UP), Howard Klaaste/Shutterstock; 8 (UP LE), Gerry Ellis/Minden Pictures; 8 (CTR), Jad Davenport/National Geographic Creative; 9 (UP), Dairon655/Dreamstime.com; 9 (LO), Windzepher/Getty Images; 10-11 (CTR), SuperStock/Alamy Stock Photo; 11 (UP), Photographs by Maria itina/Getty Images; 11 (CTR), tbkmedia.de/Alamy Stock Photo; 12 (CTR), Pete Gallop/Shutterstock; 13 (UP), Sahara Niger Tenere/SuperStock; 13 (LO), Thomas Rabeil/Nature Picture Library; 14-15 (CTR), apple2499/Shutterstock; 16 (UP), Stepan Kapl/Shutterstock; 16 (CTR), Dirk Freder/Shutterstock; 16 (LO), David Plummer/Alamy Stock Photo; 17 (UP), Denis-Huot/Nature Picture Library; 17 (CTR RT), Rod Williams/Nature Picture Library; 17 (CTR), Photononstop/Alamy Stock Photo; 17 (LO RT), Val Duncan/Kenebec Images/Alamy Stock Photo; 18 (UP), Adam Jones/Getty Images; 20-21 (RT), Danita Delimont/Alamy Stock Photo; 22 (LO), Mark Malkinson/Alamy Stock Photo; 23 (UP), Tom & Pat Leeson; 23, Eric Isselee/Shutterstock; 24 (CTR), Wegner/Nature Picture Library; 24 (LO LE), perets/Getty Images; 25 (UP), Tui De Roy/Nature Picture Library; 25 (LO), bah69/Getty Images; 26 (LO), Steve Winter/Getty Images; 27 (CTR), Neil Aldridge/Nature Picture Library; 27 (CTR), Jonelle Louw/Alamy Stock Photo; 28 (UP), Brent Stirton/National Geographic Creative; 28 (LO), epa/Alamy Stock Photo; 29 (CTR), age fotostock/Alamy Stock Photo; 30 (LO LE), RubinowaDama/Shutterstock; 30 (LO RT), Gerard Lacz/Minden Pictures; 31 (UP LE), Paul Sawer/Minden Pictures; 31 (UP RT), Mikhail Turkeev/Shutterstock; 31 (LO LE), Gerry Ellis/Minden Pictures; 32 (LO RT), George Sanker/Nature Picture Library; 32 (UP RT), Jad Davenport/National Geographic Creative; 32 (UP LE), Danita Delimont/Alamy Stock Photo; Vocab (throughout), Gisele Yashar/Shutterstock; Header (throughout), RAYphotog/Shutterstock

Table of Contents

Meet the Cats

Wild cats aren't like house cats. Most wild cats live in wild places. They're found all over the world.

Scientists have counted 35 species of wild cats.

Let's meet some!

Fur Word

SPECIES: A group of related living things

Some wild cats are called big cats. This lion is a big cat. So are tigers, leopards, and jaguars.

Cats of the World

Some wild cats live in open grasslands. They're fast and powerful. They must be quick to chase animals across the grass.

African wildcat

serval

cheetahs

Margays live in the lush rain forests of Central America.

Wild cats also live in jungles and forests. Some are good at climbing trees. Many jungle cats enjoy swimming. Sometimes they even catch fish!

tiger

jaguars

Wild cats can be found in the cold, too. They often live in snowy mountains.

snow leopard

These cats have thick fur to keep them warm. Their wide paws act like snowshoes.

A Eurasian lynx has thick fur on its wide feet. This helps it walk in deep snow.

sand cat

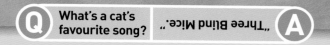

Only one type of wild cat makes its home in the desert. Meet the sand cat. It can live for months without drinking. It gets water from the food it eats.

Sand cats eat insects, birds, and even snakes!

A Cat Up Close

Wild cats live in many different habitats. But they have some things in common. Let's check out the body parts that cats have.

Fur Word

HABITAT: An animal's natural home

A long tail helps most cats balance.

Ears can hear many more sounds than human ears can.

The nose has a powerful sense of smell.

Teeth are long and sharp.

Whiskers help cats find their way in the dark.

Claws curve into sharp points.

7 COOL FACTS
About Wild Cats

1

All big cats roar. They do not purr the way other wild cats do.

2

Cheetahs are the world's fastest land animals. They can reach 100 kilometres an hour in seconds.

3

Big cats don't just roar. They also make a purr-like sound called a chuffle. It's their way of saying hello.

4

Many wild cats can catch animals that are more than twice their size.

5

Rusty spotted cats are the smallest wild cats. They weigh about 1.3 kilograms. Tigers are the biggest cats. They can weigh up to 300 kilograms!

6

Sand cats have thick fur on their paws. This helps them walk in sand without sinking.

Snow leopards are great leapers. They can jump as far as 6 metres.

7

Built to Hunt

A cheetah chases its prey.

All cats eat meat. Wild cats must hunt for their food. They catch other animals.

Fur Word 🐾

PREY: An animal that is
eaten by another animal

This is hard work. Many cats
run fast and chase their prey.
Others sneak up on it.

Can you spot the cat in this picture? It's not so easy! Wild cats are great at hiding. They don't want their prey to see them and run away. Wild cats use camouflage to blend in.

Fur Word

CAMOUFLAGE: An animal's colour or pattern that helps it hide from other animals

Canada lynx

Caring for Cubs

Wild cats give birth to cubs. Young cubs drink milk from their mothers.

a tiger mother and her cub

young cougar cubs with their mother

Mothers teach their cubs how to hunt. When the cats are old enough, they go off to live on their own.

lion cub

Wild Cat Q & A

Find out the answers to these questions about wild cats!

European wildcats

WHY DO CATS SCRATCH?
Cats must keep their
claws sharp and clean.
So they scratch tree bark
like it's a scratching post.

house cat

feral cat

DO SOME HOUSE CATS LIVE IN THE WILD?
Yes, they're called feral cats. They're the same species as house cats. But they act more like wild cats.

WHY CAN'T WILD CATS LIVE IN PEOPLE'S HOMES?
Wild cats wouldn't make good pets. They need to hunt and roam large areas. They can also be dangerous.

caracal

Wild Cats and People

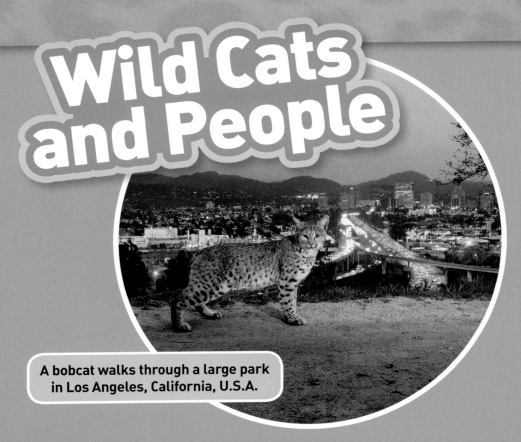

A bobcat walks through a large park in Los Angeles, California, U.S.A.

Sometimes people move into places where wild cats live. This causes problems. The cats have less space to live and hunt in the wild. They might hunt people's farm animals instead. The people want to protect their animals.

Farmers in South Africa sometimes use traps to keep wild cats away from their animals.

Helping Hands

A Maasai man tracks lions for a special program in Africa. The program helps keep people and lions safe.

An Iberian lynx is let out into the wild.

Some people are studying wild cats. This helps them learn how to protect the cats. Others are working on how to keep cats' habitats safe. We can work together to share the world with wild cats.

What in the World?

These pictures show up-close views of things in a wild cat's world. Use the hints to work out what's in the pictures. Answers are on page 31.

1

2

HINT: These help wild cats find their way in the dark.

HINT: Wild cats give birth to these.

Word Bank

claws   tail   desert   cubs   whiskers   fur

3

HINT: Wild cats keep these sharp and clean.

4

HINT: This helps a wild cat balance.

5

HINT: This keeps wild cats warm.

6

HINT: Only one type of wild cat lives here.

Answers: 1) whiskers, 2) cubs, 3) claws, 4) tail, 5) fur, 6) desert

CAMOUFLAGE: An animal's colour or pattern that helps it hide from other animals

HABITAT: An animal's natural home

PREY: An animal that is eaten by another animal

SPECIES: A group of related living things